FUN WITH SCIENCE

ENERGY AND GROWTH

ROSIE HARLOW & GARETH MORGAN

Contents

Use the symbols below to help you
identify the three kinds of practical
activities in this book.

EXPERIMENTS

GAMES

THINGS TO MAKE

Illustrated by Kuo Kang Chen • Cecilia Fitzsimmons

WARWICK PRESS

Introduction

All living things grow and reproduce. Green plants make seeds which grow into new plants. Animals produce eggs which grow into new animals. In this book you will find out the conditions that animals need in order to grow. You will discover the special conditions seeds require to germinate and you can discover why many plants make flowers before they make seeds.

Without plants there would be no animals. Plants provide the energy animals need to survive and grow. Plants also produce the oxygen that animals breathe. You can find out how the energy from the sun gets passed along to all living things.

When conditions are good, plants and animals grow quickly. When conditions are harsh, growth is much slower. You can find how animals survive these conditions.

By doing the experiments and playing the games in this book you will be able to find the answers to the questions on these two pages.

This book covers eight main topics:
- What a seed is and how it germinates
- How seeds move from place to place
- Flowers and insects
- How plants use water and what happens if they cannot find it
- How plants use sunlight
- How animals grow
- Surviving attacks by predators and using camouflage
- How humans can help

A blue line (like the one around the edge of these two pages) indicates the start of a new topic.

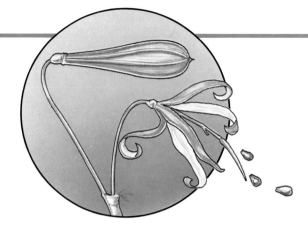

▲How do seeds get around? (page 8)

▼Do all plants make flowers? (page 15)

▼What do plants need to grow? (page 16)

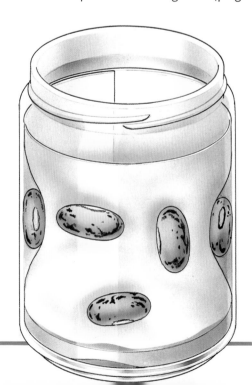

► How do animals grow? (page 29)

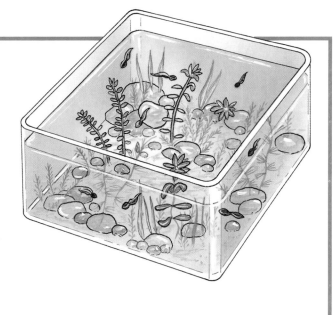

▼ Where do plants store energy? (page 24)

▲Why is light so important? (page 22)

▲ How do animals and plants survive in difficult conditions? (page 35)

► How can you help animals to survive? (page 38)

Seeds and Germination

A huge oak tree starts life as an acorn half an inch long. An apple tree grows from a little pip. All green plants start life as a small seed. These experiments will help you discover more about seeds and how they grow.

▲ Not all plants grow rooted to the ground. The plants here are living up a tree and getting all they need to grow from the air.

Experiments With Seeds

Seeds need certain conditions before they can start to grow, or **germinate**. These experiments will help you decide what these conditions might be.

Put cotton balls or tissue paper into each of the cups and some seeds on top. Each of the cups will be given different conditions which might help the seeds to germinate.

Cup 1: Sprinkle with water each day and keep on a light windowsill.
Cup 2: Keep on a windowsill — but add no water.
Cup 3: Make sure the seeds are firmly held in the tissue paper. Fill up the cup with water that has been boiled and left to cool.
Cup 4: Sprinkle with water each day and keep in a refrigerator.
Cup 5: Sprinkle with water each day and keep in a dark box in a warm place.

Look at the seeds each day for a week. Which factors help seeds to germinate — light, water, warmth, air?

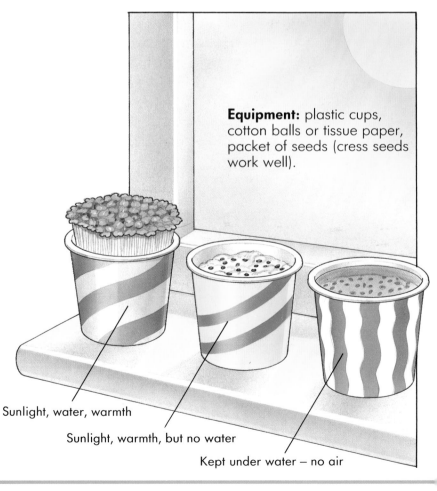

Equipment: plastic cups, cotton balls or tissue paper, packet of seeds (cress seeds work well).

Sunlight, water, warmth

Sunlight, warmth, but no water

Kept under water – no air

Fun With Seeds

- Put some tissue paper into a saucer and dampen it. Arrange seeds on the paper in the shape of your initials. Keep the seeds damp and warm and watch the letters grow.
- Next time you eat a boiled egg keep the egg shell. Put some cotton inside, add some seeds and water them. The egg will start to grow "hair," and you can draw a face on it. After a while you can cut the "hair" and eat the cress.

Ancient Seeds

Seeds can lie dormant for hundreds of years before sprouting. It has even been claimed that seeds from Egyptian tombs have germinated after thousands of years.

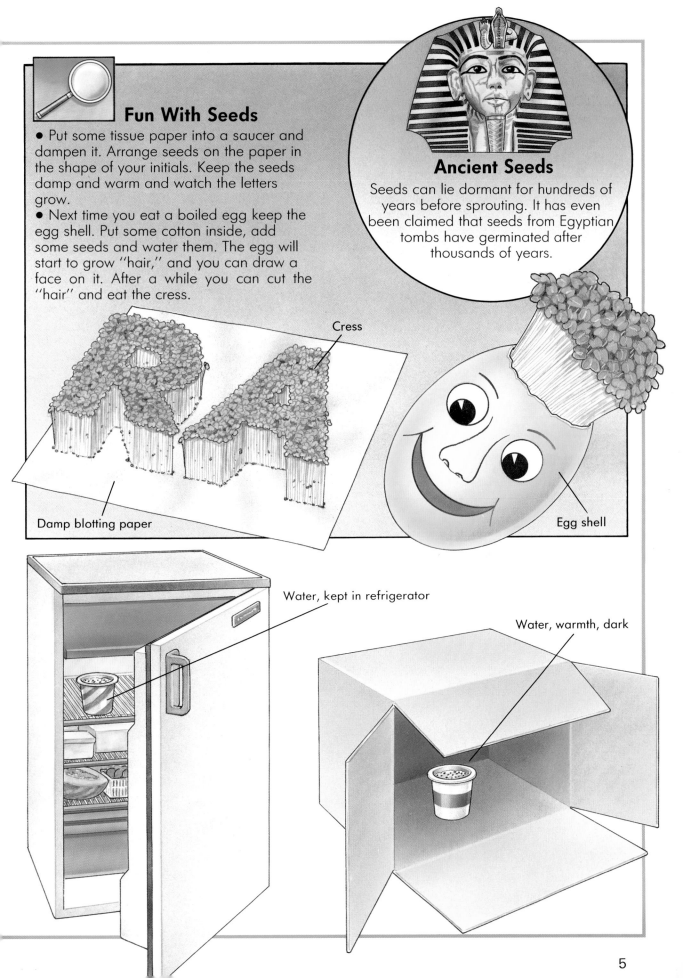

Cress

Damp blotting paper

Egg shell

Water, kept in refrigerator

Water, warmth, dark

What Is a Seed?

Seeds need air, water, and warmth to germinate. For a seed to germinate, it needs these things in the right order. This section explores how germination is most likely to occur. You can also find out how to germinate some seeds that you can eat, and some that will grow into flowers.

Make Your Own Seeds

Place a small seed, such as a cress seed, side-by-side with a grain of sand. In some ways they look rather similar. However, the sand will remain as a tiny grain, while the seed contains all the information needed to let it develop into a plant.

The Germination Game

You need six information tickets to go inside the seed. Write instructions on each ticket as follows:
1. Start to take in water
2. Start to take in oxygen
3. Use up stored food to start growing
4. Send out root
5. Send out shoot
6. Make new food in the leaves

Your seed is now ready to germinate. First you must throw a 1 with a die. Take out ticket 1. Now the seed can start to take in water — it has started to germinate. You must now throw a 2 for the next ticket, then a 3. When you throw a 4 you can attach the root to the seed. Then a 5 means you can attach the shoot. Finally you must score the 6, and the seed will have germinated successfully.

You must throw the numbers in the right order. All the stages in germination must happen in the right order. All the information needed to germinate is contained within a tiny seed, but it can only do so if the outside conditions are suitable.

Blow-up the balloon. Tear the newspaper into strips. Paste the strips onto the balloon until the paper is about four pieces thick. Leave the balloon to dry overnight. When it is dry, cut a hole about 3 inches at one end. You can now paint the seed.

The seed has a hard coat to keep out water and disease.

Make a leaf from paper. The plant needs leaves to make food.

Information tickets

Make a yellow root. The plant needs a root to take in water and minerals.

Germinate Some Seeds

You may be surprised how many seeds you can find in your kitchen. Some of these will germinate, although some have been treated so they can't. Put some blotting paper on a plate and spread some seeds on top. Make sure this is kept damp each day. If the seeds germinate they will be ready to eat after three days to a week. They can also be grown in a jar with muslin over the top. Try some of the following kitchen seeds and find out which germinate: lentils, rice, or mung beans.

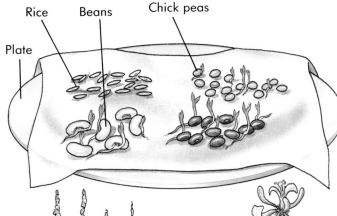

Plate · Rice · Beans · Chick peas

An Indoor Vegetable Garden

Many of the vegetables we eat are grown from seed, and you can easily grow some of these yourself. Half fill a tray with potting compost and make it damp, but not soggy. Make lines across the compost with a stick and tip the seeds along the lines. Cover the seeds up again. Leave the tray somewhere warm and light and check each day that it is damp. Cress will grow quickly and can be cut with scissors to eat in salads. If the other plants come up too thickly move them to another tray made up in the same way.

Equipment: plastic tray, potting compost, packets of vegetable seeds e.g. radish, cress, lettuce, flower seeds e.g. nasturtium, marigold.

Cress · Lettuce · Radish · Tray

Seeds On the Move

Next time you eat an apple, take the core apart and count how many seeds or pips there are inside. Imagine what would happen if all the apple pips in the windfall apples under an apple tree grew into new trees. Now try to calculate how many seeds a tree with 100 apples might make each year.

Not all seeds grow into new plants — try the calculation under the picture of the apple tree to find out what would happen if they all did. Many seeds land in a place where they cannot germinate, or are eaten by animals, and eventually they die. Even after germinating, the plant is not safe — daisy plants growing in a lawn are regularly mown before they get a chance to grow fully.

It is important that a plant scatters its seeds over a wide area. This is called the **dispersal** of seeds. Some ways this is done are illustrated below. Certain seeds have little hooked hairs which stick onto animal fur or clothing. Many seeds are hidden within attractive fruits so that birds eat them.

Hooking onto animals

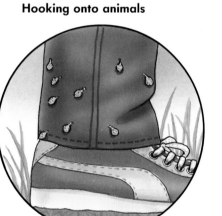

Spread by wind

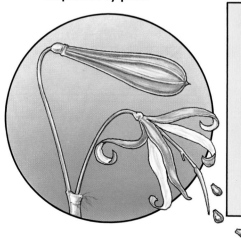

Damp potting compost

Muddy shoe

Spread by birds

Dispersed by plant

Automatic Collection

Next time you go for a walk, find out if you have been helping seeds to disperse. Scrape the mud from your shoes into a tray of potting compost and see if any plants grow. If they do you picked up seeds as you walked.

Flowers and Seeds

Plants **reproduce** (make more of themselves) by making lots of seeds. A few of these seeds germinate if the conditions are right, and grow into new plants. Apple pips, acorns, rice, and mung beans are all seeds. This section examines how a plant makes a seed so that when it dies there are new plants to take its place.

▶ Look at this picture of poppies. The seeds are forming in the pods at the center of the flowers.

Sunflowers can grow to 12 feet and have disk flowers which come in many colors. Oil is extracted from their seeds.

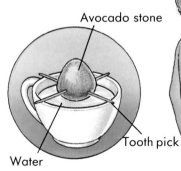

Avocado stone

Tooth pick

Water

Many other seeds can be used to grow plants at home. Try an avocado stone supported in a container of water. Pips and stones from all sorts of fruits can be grown.

The Seed Cycle

As a flower dies, the seeds start to form. These seeds can grow into new plants, which in turn make more flowers. When these die, more seeds are made again. This is known as a cycle and many events in nature occur in cycles. The seasons for example, and day and night. The seed cycle can take a very long time. If you plant an acorn it will be many years before the oak tree is old enough to make more acorns. However, you can watch the cycle happening much more quickly by using plant seeds. Sow some sunflower seeds indoors in damp potting compost during the spring. Remember to water them. When the weather becomes warm, plant the sunflower seedlings near a wall or fence which gets lots of sunshine. Put a tall stick in the ground to support the plant as it grows. Mark the stick each week to show how fast the plant is growing. Sunflowers can reach several feet in height. Once the plant has flowered, the seeds form and you can collect these to grow some more plants the following year.

Flowers and Insects

Before a flower can make seeds it must be pollinated. Look at flowers outside on a warm day. You will usually find insects buzzing around them. It is very important that insects visit flowers because if pollination does not happen seeds will not form. Flowers try to make themselves attractive to insects in many ways.

Flowers and Colors

Bees can see certain colors well. Flowers have bright petals to encourage bees to visit. Many flowers have patterns on the inside of the petals which help the bee find the nectar. They are called honey guides and are often visible as strips of color that lead into the center of the flower where the nectar is stored. They are rather like runway landing lights which guide airplanes safely onto the ground. Some honey guides only show up in ultraviolet light.

Why Do Insects Visit Flowers?

Look at a bee or a butterfly as it visits a flower. Can you see its long **proboscis** (mouthpart)? The proboscis is stuck deep into the flower. You can discover what the insect is looking for by finding a flower of the white dead-nettle. Don't confuse it with a stinging nettle! Pull the flower from the plant, and gently squeeze along the tube toward the base of the flower. A small drop of nectar should appear. Taste the sweetness on your tongue. If there is no nectar, perhaps a bee has already taken it.

Flowers Smell Nice . . .

Flowers advertise themselves with smell as well as with color. You can capture these lovely smells by making pot pourri. Ask if you can collect some petals from garden flowers. Rose petals are good for this. Dry them in a warm place and put them in a small bowl.

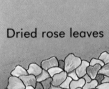

Dried rose leaves

. . . and Nasty

Some flowers are pollinated by insects other than bees. Flies normally feed on dead and rotting material so flowers that need to attract flies for pollination make smells like bad meat. While the flies are investigating what they think is a tasty meal they pick up pollen and later transfer it to other flowers.

White dead-nettle

Honeysuckle

What are Flowers For?

Flowers are the part of the plant that help to make sure that the plant reproduces and that the next generation of that plant is produced. Flowers contain the pollen and ova which together can make seeds which will grow into new plants.

Looking Inside a Flower

Every flower contains a range of very complicated structures, each with its own function to perform. The basic structures are shown below. To discover these for yourself, pick a common flower and cut it in half. You will then be able to see all the contents, such as the stamen, style, sepals, and petals. If it is a flower that is fertilized by insects you will see the nectary at the base of the flower, where the insects seek out food.

A daisy is made up of many tiny flowers. They make a large landing platform for calling insects. These pick up pollen as they wander about the flower.

Foxgloves are pollinated by large bumble bees. The flower is shaped like a bell, the bee crawls inside to collect the nectar, and picks up pollen as it does so.

Yellow flowers such as the buttercup are a particular favorite of many small insects. Try wearing yellow clothes on a sunny day and see if insects visit you.

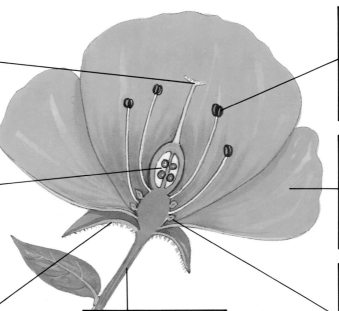

Stigma
This is the female part of the flower. When the pollen brushes off onto the stigma, pollination occurs.

Ovary
A pollen grain on the stigma grows down to the ovary. If it enters the ovary fertilization occurs and a seed develops.

Sepals
These make a tough protective cover for the delicate flower to prevent damage when it is still in bud.

Stamen
The anthers contain pollen. Pollen sticks to insects when they visit, and is taken off to another flower.

Petals
The flower advertises itself to insects by having bright petals. Petals advertise that nectar is inside.

Nectaries
Where nectar is made. Without nectar insects would not visit, and pollination could not occur.

Stem
The stem needs to be strong enough to hold up the flower.

Make a Flower

Equipment: green and yellow colored paper (or paper and paints), sticky tape, green bendy straw.

The best way to find out how a flower works is to make one yourself. You can even pollinate this model flower yourself.
Trace the shape of each part of the flower onto cardboard. You will require five petals, five sepals, one stigma, six anthers, two leaves.

1. Poke the straw through the middle of the sepals.
2. Push the narrow end of the petals into the end of the straw. You may find it easier if you fold the narrow part of the petal down the middle first.
3. Push the stigma into the straw in the same way.
4. Arrange the anthers in a circle around the stigma by pushing them into the straw too.
5. Tape the leaves to the lower part of the stem.

   You can make different model flowers by changing the color and number of petals. You can also vary the length and number of anthers and styles. There are many possible variations on the same basic idea. There are thousands of different flowers, and the next page will help you to identify some of them.

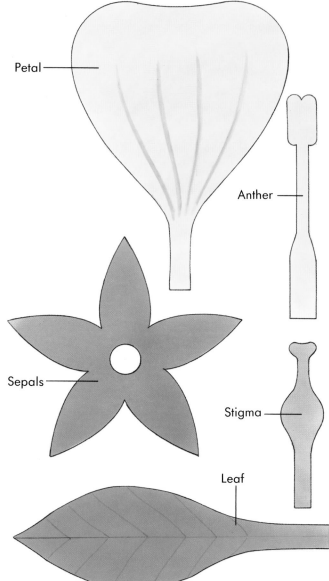

Petal

Anther

Sepals

Stigma

Leaf

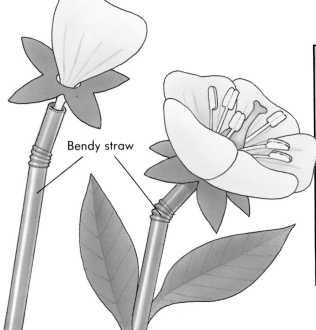

Bendy straw

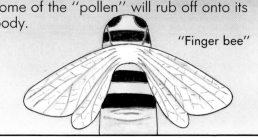

Pollinate Your Flower

Balance a small amount of baking flour on the anthers. Make your finger into a bee by painting it as shown. Put a small drop of honey right inside the flower to represent nectar. As it enters the flower, some of the "pollen" will rub off onto its body.

"Finger bee"

A Wild Flower Hunt

Flowers come in many shapes and sizes. However, most of them need to attract insects to visit so pollination can occur. Many flowers have strange names because of the way they look, or because of stories that are told about them. People used to think that foxgloves were worn by foxes.

If you want to identify a flower, start off by making a flower chart. Draw a picture of the flower in the center of a piece of paper, and fill out the information around the edge.

Number of flowers on stem
One

Shape of leaf

How many anthers?
Five

Is it alone or are there lots together?
Lots together

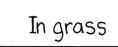 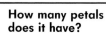
How many stigmas?
Two

How big is the flower?
One inch across

Where is it?
In grass

How high is it off the ground?
Four inches

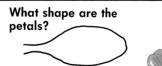
How many petals does it have?
Four

What does it smell of?
Like apples

What color is it?
Blue

What shape are the petals?

Pressing and Drying Flowers

The best method for pressing flowers is to place a clean sheet of paper in a large book and lay the flower on this. Cover it with a large piece of blotting paper and close the book. Pile other large books on top and your flower will be ready after a month. Some flowers can be dried without pressing. Hang these up in a bunch somewhere warm. Many wild flowers are protected by law. Use garden flowers unless you are sure a wild flower is very common.

Blotting paper

Pile of heavy books

Flowers Without Petals

Many flowers are fertilized by insects. Some flowers are fertilized in other ways so they don't need bright petals. There are likely to be seeds made from these flowers in your kitchen, and others close to your home. Grind your own flour.

Grind Your Own Flour

Grind the wheat underneath the pestle and remove the husks as they rise to the top.

A Grass Hunt

There are thousands of different sorts of grasses, and they are pollinated by the wind and not by insects. The seeds which develop are sometimes called grains. Next time you visit some rough grassland collect a variety of grass flowers and see if any match the shape of the ones shown. Although there are no petals or sepals, you may find feathery anthers and hairy stigmas.

Grasses In the Kitchen

The cereals farmers grow for food were developed from wild grasses. The names and shapes of some wild grasses make this clear – for example, rye grass, false oat grass.

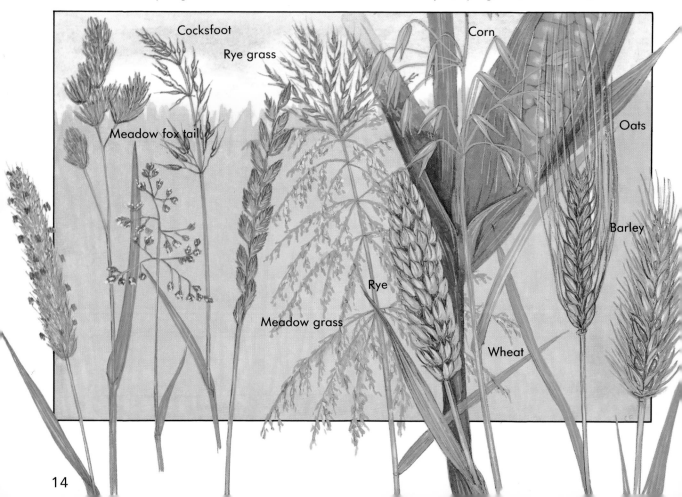

Plants Without Flowers

You might think that many of these plants don't look much like plants at all. They don't have leaves and roots, and they never have flowers. This page tells you where to find them, and how to grow them.

Algae under microscope

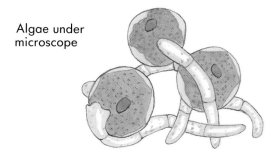

If the water in a pond is green it is usually because of millions of tiny green algae. Even magnified many times each one still looks like a tiny green blob. However, algae have an excellent way of making more algae. Each one in the water can split into two more, then each of the two algae formed can grow again. These can each divide into two new algae, and so on.

▲ Gravestones are a good place to look for lichens. The bigger a lichen the older it is, so look for them on the oldest headstones.

Lichens are fungi and algae growing together, and they reproduce by making spores. Look for lichens on trees, old walls, and stones. They often look like flat pancakes and may be gray, green, or orange. If you find many near you it means the air is clean. If there are few, the pollution in the air has killed many of them.

Grow Some Algae

You can grow algae by placing a clear container of rain water on a sunny window-sill for a few days. The water will turn green as **spores** (seeds) of algae from the air quickly grow and divide.

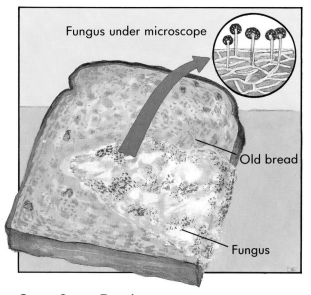

Grow Some Fungi

Put an old piece of bread on some plastic and keep it damp for a few days. Look to see if gray or blue patches appear. These are fungi, developing from spores that have landed from the air.

From Seed to Plant

Seeds require certain conditions to germinate. In this section you can find out what conditions a plant needs to grow after it has germinated. Here are some suggestions as to what a plant might require in order to grow: air, water, soil, gravity, light, fertilizer, and darkness.

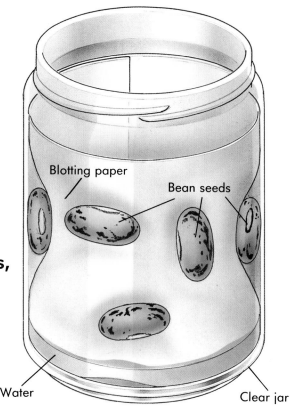

Blotting paper

Bean seeds

Water

Clear jar

Does Gravity Affect Seeds, Roots, and Shoots?

The shoot of a plant will grow toward the light. However, seeds may be buried deep in the soil when they start to grow. This experiment examines whether a seed planted upside down grows downward with its roots in the air.

Tape blotting paper into a jar as shown. Pour some water into the jar so that the blotting paper can soak it up. Place some beans between the paper and the jar in a variety of different positions; use a pencil to help. Place the jar in a completely dark place and look at it each day. You will find that the roots still grow downward and the shoot upward. When there is no light the shoot responds to gravity. This is necessary because the seed is in darkness before the shoot emerges into the sunlight.

1 All around light

2 Kept in dark

3 Light from one side

4 Aluminum foil cap

Do Plants Need Light?

Equipment: four jars or plastic cups, broad bean seeds, cotton balls, aluminum foil.

Put cotton in each of the jars, and make it wet. Place two bean seeds in each cup.

Check the seeds each day, and keep the cotton damp. Place the cups as follows:
1. In a place with light coming from all directions.
2. In a dark closet (or make a dark tube to cover it).
3. On a sunny windowsill.
4. As 3, but make a small foil cap to place over the shoot.

Does the Color of Light Matter?

Equipment: small margarine or yogurt boxes, tissue paper, sheets of colored plastic or cellophane (e.g. clear, red, green), packet of cress seeds.

Put some damp paper in the bottom of each box. Add some seeds, and place some colored plastic over each box. Place in a warm, light place. Check the boxes each day and water if necessary. Watch to see if the color of light reaching the seedlings affects how they develop.

Clear plastic

Cress

Plastic tub

Colored plastic

Green Plants Need Light

Seeds don't need light to germinate, and they can grow without light — at least for a while. But without light they can't turn green. This is because when there is no light they cannot make the green chemical **chlorophyll** in their leaves. Because it is so important for a plant to find the light, the tip of the shoot is able to detect where the light is coming from. The plant can then grow toward the light. Without chlorophyll the plant cannot make any vital sugars and growth cannot take place. The shoot remains stunted.

► Plants always grow toward the light. This is important to trees in a wood, otherwise they would get shaded out by their neighbors.

Plants and Water

Gravity causes the roots of a plant to grow downward. The roots anchor the plant into the soil, and they also absorb water. This section looks at how much water a plant contains, how much it uses in a day, and how the water is moved around the plant. You can find out what happens to this water.

Equipment: rice, cucumber, weighing scales, baking tray, baking paper.

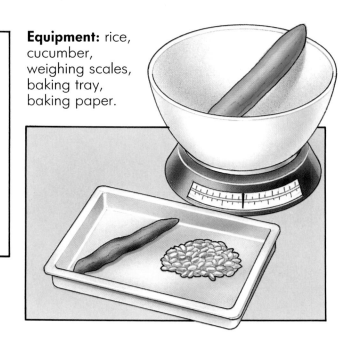

Water in Plants

Slice up some cucumber and weigh it on some baking paper. Measure the same weight of rice onto some more paper. Put them both on a baking tray along with some water in a jar top. Ask for the tray to go in the oven on a low heat. When the oven has cooled look at the water in the jar top. If the tray has been in long enough the water will have evaporated. Look at the cucumber and the rice and weigh them to see if they have lost water and become lighter.

How Does the Water Move Around?

Pour about half an inch of water into the jar. Add a teaspoonful of red coloring and mix. Break off a piece of celery at the base and place it in the red water. Look at the celery each day to see where the red water goes. How long does it take to reach the leaf? After a few days cut the celery stalk into two and look for the red stain. It should be clear where you have cut across the tubes which carry the water up the stalk. The water rises by capilliary action. The smaller the tube, the higher the level. Put twp straws in the glass, one thin, one wide. See in which the water rises farther.

Equipment: glass of water, stick of celery, red food coloring, dishwashinng liquid, straws of varying widths (or an empty tube from an old ballpoint pen).

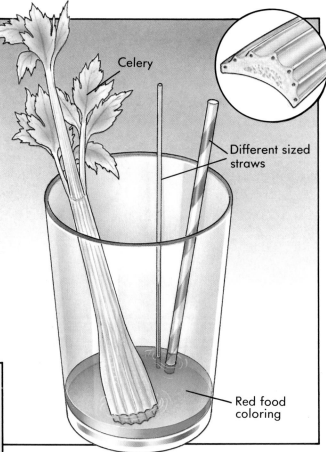

Celery

Different sized straws

Red food coloring

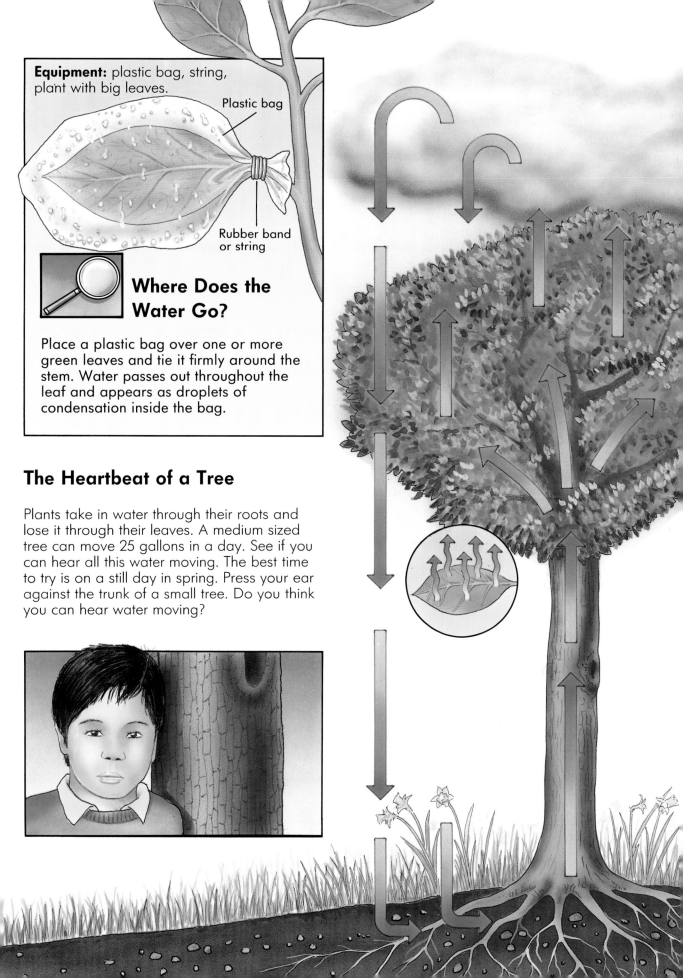

Equipment: plastic bag, string, plant with big leaves.

Plastic bag

Rubber band or string

Where Does the Water Go?

Place a plastic bag over one or more green leaves and tie it firmly around the stem. Water passes out throughout the leaf and appears as droplets of condensation inside the bag.

The Heartbeat of a Tree

Plants take in water through their roots and lose it through their leaves. A medium sized tree can move 25 gallons in a day. See if you can hear all this water moving. The best time to try is on a still day in spring. Press your ear against the trunk of a small tree. Do you think you can hear water moving?

Green Deserts

When a forest is chopped down the water cycle is broken. The rain is no longer taken up by the trees and there are no roots to hold the soil. Often the soil is washed away and the area turns into a desert. Because there are no trees, transpiration does not occur, and clouds can't form in the dry air. In many parts of the world deserts are getting bigger as more and more trees are cut down. The water cycle can be started up again, however. Tough trees can be planted in the deserts to hold the soil and start cycling the water again.

▶ Desert plants have to survive on very little water. They have very long roots to tap deep water sources, which helps to move water from the soil into the atmosphere.

Leaves Give Off Something Else

Equipment: small jar of water, a funnel, a bottle to go over the funnel, Canadian pondweed.

Arrange the equipment as shown. The bottle upside down over the funnel must be full of water. You may find this easier by setting up the experiment under water in a sink. Start the experiment in bright light, and watch to see if bubbles start forming. Move the experiment to a shady place and see if the bubbles appear more or less quickly. The bubbles coming off consist of a most important gas. This gas is **oxygen** and it is given off by all green leaves. Oxygen is one of the gases in the air all around you, and it is the one your body absorbs when you breathe in. All animals need oxygen to stay alive. This is another reason why plants are so important. If there were no plants there would be no oxygen to breathe.

If a glowing splint relights in a jar of gas, the gas is oxygen. Ask an adult to try this for you.

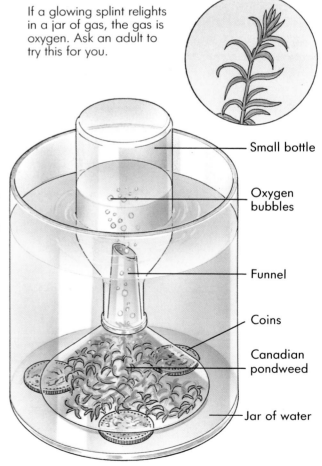

- Small bottle
- Oxygen bubbles
- Funnel
- Coins
- Canadian pondweed
- Jar of water

A Bottle Garden

Equipment: large plastic jar with lid, gravel, soil, small plants (see below).

The water transpiring from a leaf becomes visible when a bag is put over it. This **condensed** water can be used again by the plant if it is absorbed through the roots. This bottle garden uses water in this way. Put some gravel or small stones in the jar and lay it on its side. Add a layer of damp soil or compost. Choose some small plants from a garden or a nursery. Some ideas are illustrated but ask for advice. Press the plants into the soil with a long stick, and attach the lid tightly. Put the jar in a light place, but not in direct sunlight. The plants in the bottle use the water in the soil and the carbon dioxide in the air to make sugar. They give off oxygen as they do this. At night when there is no light to help photosynthesis the plants use the energy in their food stores, they respire.

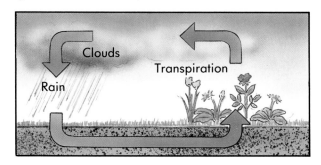

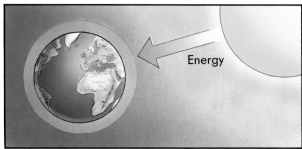

A cycle in the bottle

Our earth relies on a water cycle. The plants transpire water which condenses as clouds. The water falls back as rain which the plants can use again.

Bottle garden maintenance

Make sure that you keep the bottle garden clean. Put it in a light place and somewhere reasonably cool. Make sure the lid fits tightly.

A cycle in the Earth

The total amount of water on earth is nearly constant. No water arrives or leaves. There is only one thing which reaches the earth from outside and that is sunlight.

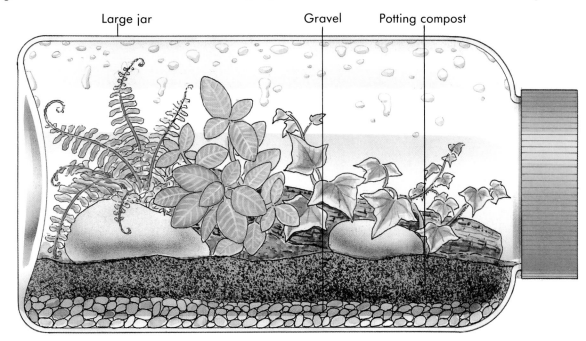

Large jar   Gravel   Potting compost

Green Energy

The last section showed that plants need water and sunlight, and that they give off oxygen. In this section you can find out what they use the sunlight for, and what happens if plants are kept in the dark. You will find out that oxygen is not the only thing that plants make which we need.

Plants In the Dark

For this experiment you will need a brick with a dip in one side. Place the brick with the dip face down on an area of green grass (but ask an adult first as this will spoil the lawn!). Each day carefully look under the brick and then replace it in exactly the same place. Compare the grass underneath the brick with the rest of the lawn. The grass will go yellow because it was hidden from the light.

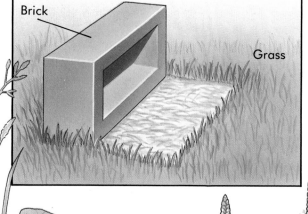

Brick

Grass

Food Producers

Animals obtain their energy to live and grow by eating. Green plants have to make their own food. They do this in their leaves. The green chemical in the leaves is called **chlorophyll**. It is the chlorophyll which converts sunlight energy into food energy. It does this by combining water (taken in by the roots) and carbon dioxide gas (taken in through the leaves) to form sugars. When there is no light, sugars cannot be made, and eventually the plant will die.

As the sugars are produced, oxygen is formed as a waste product and is given out by the leaf along with surplus water. So plants are vital to us in two ways. They give out oxygen for us to breathe, and they make food energy which we can eat.

Sunlight

Food traveling
down plant from
leaves

Which Plants Like the Light?

Throw the hoop a short way over your shoulder. Record how many different kinds of plant there are inside your hoop, and identify any if you can. Try and record if there are different types of grass or only one. You will find that some plants prefer the shade, some prefer light areas.

Equipment: a hoop.

Did You Know?

Some plants do not make their own food, or make only a limited amount. They are called parasitic plants. They attach suckers to the stems or roots of another plant and steal the food that it makes. Some other plants supplement their food by eating insects. Different species use hinged leaves, sticky hairs, or long, waxed funnels to catch their prey. The insect is slowly dissolved in the plant's digestive fluids.

23

Plants Store Food

The food a plant makes is transported around the plant to where it is needed. However, the plant may not need energy straight away, so the food must be stored. This reserve of food may be used later for a variety of reasons: to help the plant survive the winter, or to assist in the formation of seeds and fruits. Animals and people can eat much of the food that plants store.

Vegetable Food Sources

The sugars made in the leaves can be stored as sugar, or converted into other high energy substances like fats or carbohydrates. Eat some lettuce leaves and try to decide if they contain much sugar or carbohydrate. Various parts of a plant can be used to store food, for example the root or the stem.

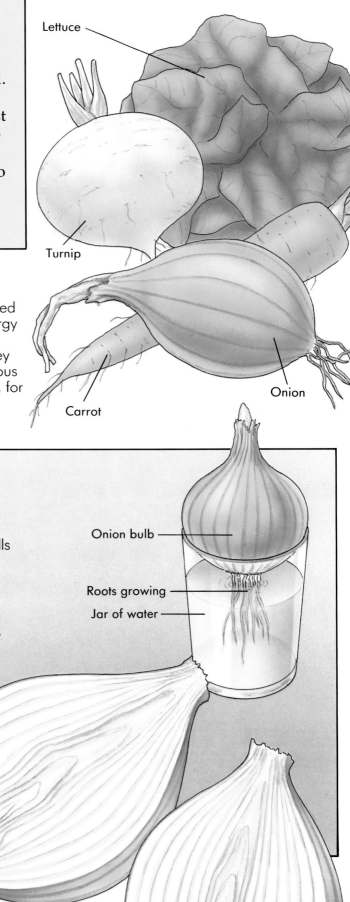

Lettuce

Turnip

Carrot

Onion

Cut Up an Onion

Each of the "shells" in an onion is a swollen leaf. You can show that these shells are leaves by letting an old onion grow. Rest it on a jar full of water and watch it develop. Roots will grow from the hard bottom part — this is the tiny stem — and the top of the swollen leaves will start to shoot. At the same time the onion "shells" will start to shrivel as the food in them is used up.

Onion bulb

Roots growing

Jar of water

Swollen base of leaf

Onion cut in two

Why Do Plants Store Food?

Plants store food in roots (carrots), stems (potatoes) and leaves (onions). What is this food used for? The experiment with the onion shows that the stored food can be used to start the plant growing again. This is useful after the winter because all the growing parts of the plant have died back. When the warm weather starts the plant can grow up again quickly using the stored food energy. So a plant with stored food has an advantage over a plant growing from seed.

Grow a Carrot Top
Use a carrot top that still has leaves. Put it in water or wet cotton and look for new roots forming.

▲ The exact food stored varies from plant to plant. Potatoes store food as starch. Much of the sugar we eat comes from sugar beet.

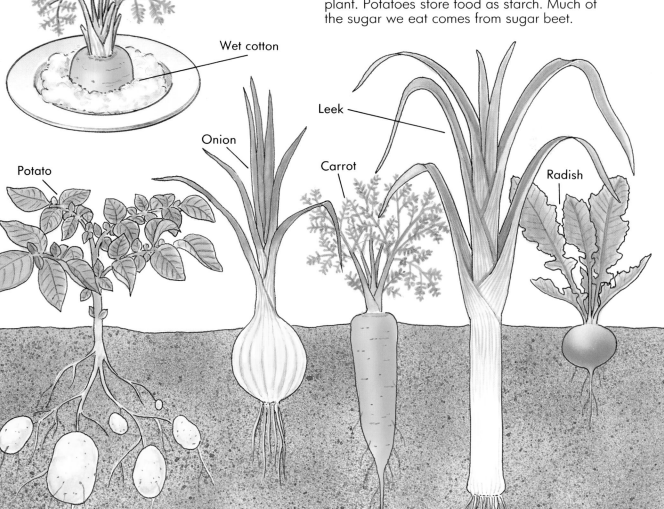

Carrot top

Wet cotton

Leek

Onion

Carrot

Radish

Potato

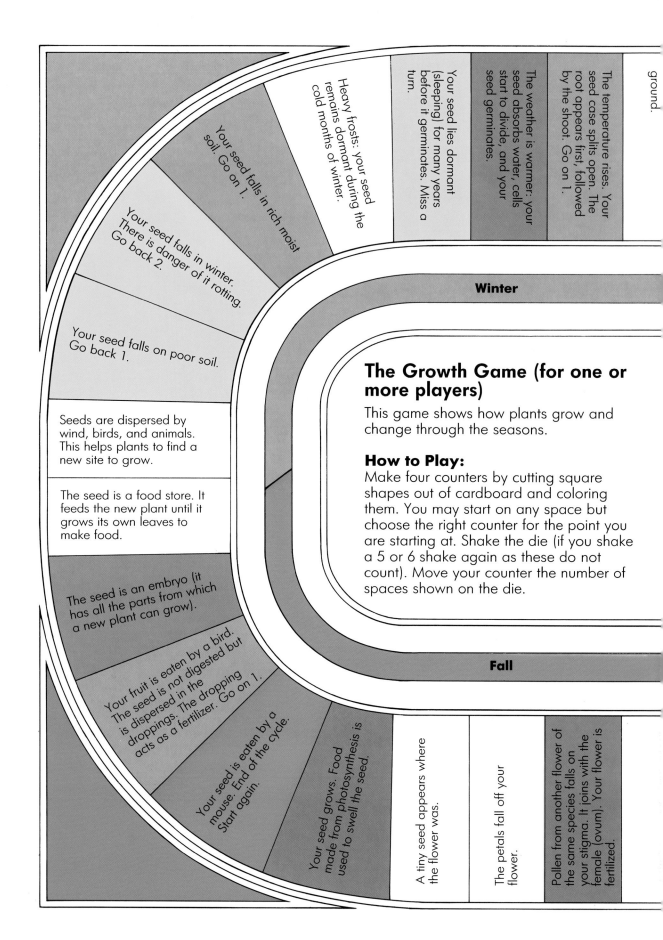

ground.

The temperature rises. Your seed case splits open. The root appears first, followed by the shoot. Go on 1.

The weather is warmer: your seed absorbs water, cells start to divide, and your seed germinates.

Your seed lies dormant (sleeping) for many years before it germinates. Miss a turn.

Heavy frosts: your seed remains dormant during the cold months of winter.

Your seed falls in rich moist soil. Go on 1.

Your seed falls in winter. There is danger of it rotting. Go back 2.

Your seed falls on poor soil. Go back 1.

Seeds are dispersed by wind, birds, and animals. This helps plants to find a new site to grow.

The seed is a food store. It feeds the new plant until it grows its own leaves to make food.

The seed is an embryo (it has all the parts from which a new plant can grow).

Your fruit is eaten by a bird. The seed is not digested but is dispersed in the droppings. The dropping acts as a fertilizer. Go on 1.

Your seed is eaten by a mouse. End of the cycle. Start again.

Your seed grows. Food made from photosynthesis is used to swell the seed.

A tiny seed appears where the flower was.

The petals fall off your flower.

Pollen from another flower of the same species falls on your stigma. It joins with the female (ovum). Your flower is fertilized.

Winter

Fall

The Growth Game (for one or more players)

This game shows how plants grow and change through the seasons.

How to Play:

Make four counters by cutting square shapes out of cardboard and coloring them. You may start on any space but choose the right counter for the point you are starting at. Shake the die (if you shake a 5 or 6 shake again as these do not count). Move your counter the number of spaces shown on the die.

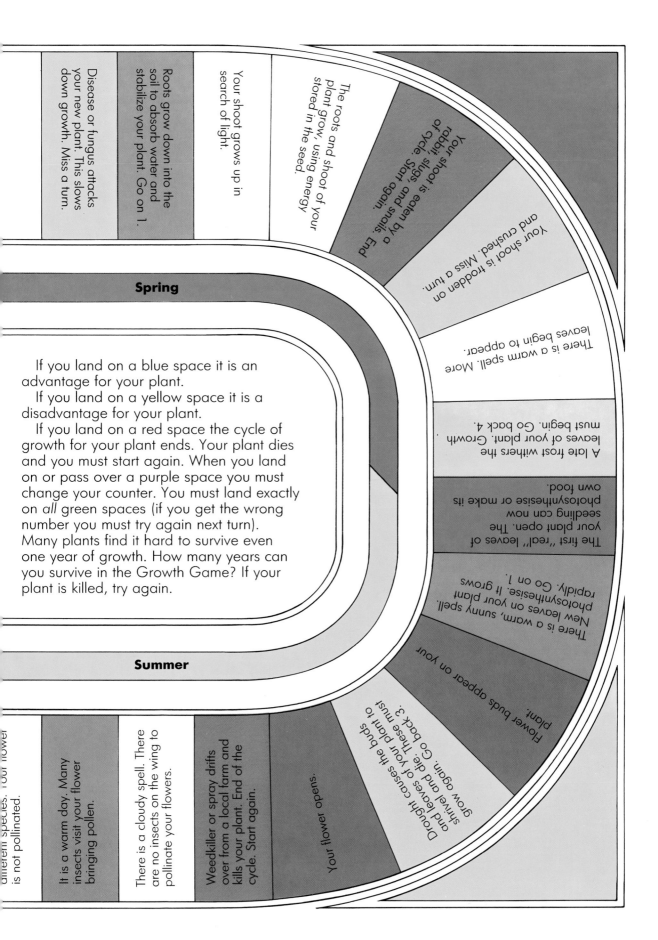

Spring

Disease or fungus attacks your new plant. This slows down growth. Miss a turn.

Roots grow down into the soil to absorb water and stabilize your plant. Go on 1.

Your shoot grows up in search of light.

The roots and shoot of your plant grow, using energy stored in the seed.

Your shoot is eaten by a rabbit, slug, and snails. End of cycle. Start again.

Your shoot is trodden on and crushed. Miss a turn.

There is a warm spell. More leaves begin to appear.

A late frost withers the leaves of your plant. Growth must begin. Go back 4.

The first "real" leaves of your plant open. The seedling can now photosynthesise or make its own food.

There is a warm, sunny spell. New leaves on your plant photosynthesise. It grows rapidly. Go on 1.

Flower buds appear on your plant.

If you land on a blue space it is an advantage for your plant.

If you land on a yellow space it is a disadvantage for your plant.

If you land on a red space the cycle of growth for your plant ends. Your plant dies and you must start again. When you land on or pass over a purple space you must change your counter. You must land exactly on *all* green spaces (if you get the wrong number you must try again next turn). Many plants find it hard to survive even one year of growth. How many years can you survive in the Growth Game? If your plant is killed, try again.

Summer

Drought causes the buds to shrivel and die. These must grow again. Go back 3.

Your flower opens.

different species. Your flower is not pollinated.

It is a warm day. Many insects visit your flower bringing pollen.

There is a cloudy spell. There are no insects on the wing to pollinate your flowers.

Weedkiller or spray drifts over from a local farm and kills your plant. End of the cycle. Start again.

How Animals Grow

Different creatures grow at different rates. A rabbit becomes adult when it is only four months old. An Aphid can grow up in three days. Human beings may still be growing after 15 years. Young animals sometimes look like a small version of the adult (for example a human baby) and sometimes completely different (for example a caterpillar, which turns into a butterfly).

Look At an Egg

In one sense all animals start life as an egg. In some cases the young animal has developed from the egg before the mother gives birth. Mammals, including humans, are an example of this. With other animals, the egg has a protective covering and is laid by the mother. The young animal develops inside the egg and then hatches out. Crack open a chicken's egg into a saucer and see if you can find the parts marked on the left-hand diagram.

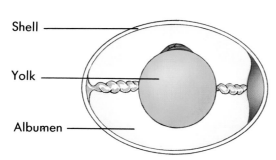

Shell
Yolk
Albumen

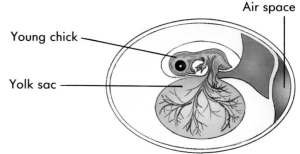

Air space
Young chick
Yolk sac

Look for the "blood spot." This is the part that could develop into a chick. However, most chicken eggs have not been fertilized by the male so this cannot happen. When you boil an egg, prick it at the blunt end. It is when the air in this expands that the egg cracks.

How Snails Grow

Water snails lay eggs that are easy to see. Look for lines of jelly underneath leaves in water where they live. The tiny dots inside are the eggs. Look at them every day with a hand lens and watch the snails take shape. The eggs of garden snails are hard to find in the wild, but easy if you keep snails at home. As young snails grow, the shells become stronger. When they are strong enough you can mark the edge of a shell with ink each week to see how fast it grows.

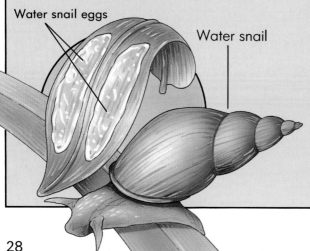

Water snail eggs
Water snail

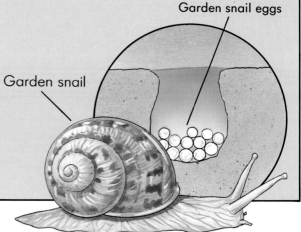

Garden snail eggs
Garden snail

How Frogs Grow

Collect a small amount of frog spawn from a pond. Make sure you have permission to do this. Keep the spawn in a large plastic tank, using water taken from the pond. Cover the tank to stop the water evaporating. Keep the tank somewhere cool, but not too cold, and out of the sun. After the tadpoles have hatched, choose a few to keep and return the rest to the pond. Tadpoles will eat algae in the tank, but as they grow they need extra nutrients. When they are big enough hang a piece of raw meat in the tank for them to eat.

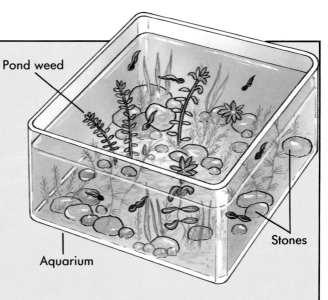

Pond weed

Stones

Aquarium

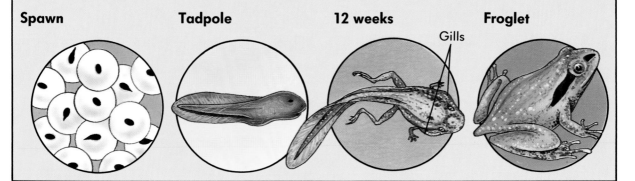

Spawn   **Tadpole**   **12 weeks**   **Froglet**

Gills

How Reptiles Grow

As a tadpole grows it changes shape entirely. This is called **metamorphosis**. You may be able to think of what sort of metamorphosis a butterfly shows as it grows from an egg. Reptiles grow in an equally surprising way. Snakes and lizards do not change shape as they grow, but shed their skins, which will only stretch so much before they have to be replaced. Each time they do this there is a new skin underneath. Many reptiles are rare, and some dangerous, so it is not a good idea to keep them as pets.

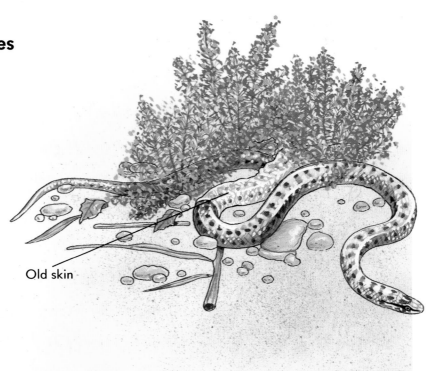

Old skin

Watching Woodlice

Woodlice belong to the same group of animals as crabs — the **crustaceans**. They are quite easy to keep, but remember that crustaceans lose water easily and so must be kept in damp surroundings. Use a plastic box with soil in the bottom; add some bark and leaves. Put in a container of water to keep the air damp. Put the woodlouse box somewhere cool and shady. Stock it with woodlice found under logs and stones. Like reptiles, woodlice shed their skins. Look under their bodies for eggs or young.

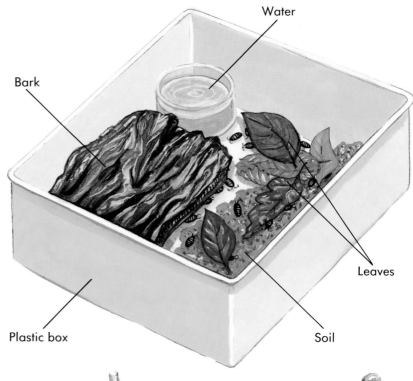

Water

Bark

Leaves

Plastic box

Soil

Keeping Stick Insects

It is possible to get hold of stick insects from pet shops, wild life parks with insect houses, and sometimes schools. Remember to ask what plants they feed on and how to look after them. Make sure you have plenty of food near your house (usually privet leaves or bramble). A large plastic jar with holes in the lid makes a good container. Be careful to clean them out and provide fresh food for them.

They are fascinating creatures to keep. Watch the way they grow by shedding their skin. Try to get a male and female so they can mate and produce young. Look out for eggs. They can take up to a month to hatch.

Plastic jar

Lid

Privet leaves

Mammals

You belong to a group of animals known as mammals. Other mammals include elephants, dogs, lions, and bats. Mammals have certain things in common. They are born alive, not as an egg. They drink milk from their mother. They have hair covering part of their body. Their blood stays at a constant warm temperature. Most other creatures, except birds, have a body temperature that changes as the temperature of the environment changes. Different mammals grow at different rates. This chart compares how a rabbit, a deer, a mole and a squirrel grow. You could try drawing up a similar chart for other mammals, like your pet, or even yourself.

Growing Up

The chart below shows how long four different animals take to reach adulthood. Young humans take about 12–15 years to reach maturity. All the animals below are smaller and take less time.

▲ Two types of young mammal: *above* a young deer and *below* baby rabbits. Both are able to move very soon after birth.

	Mole	Deer	Squirrel	Rabbit
How long is the young animal inside the mother?	1 month	8 months	1–2 months	1 month
How many babies are born at a time	about 4	1 (sometimes 2)	3–6	About 6
How many litters can be born in a year?	usually 1	1	1 or 2	Up to 7
How many young are born in a year?	about 4	Usually 1	up to 12	10 to 20
How long does the mother suckle (give milk to) the young?	1 month	Up to a year	up to 2 months	1 month
Can the new-born mammal see?	no	Yes	no	No
Can the new-born mammal walk?	no	Yes	no	No
Does it have a good layer of fur?	no	Yes	no	No
When is it ready to leave the mother?	1 month	1 year	3 months	1 month
When is it ready to have its own young?	1 year	2 or 3 years	6 months	4 months

Food for Growth

Most plants make their own food, using carbon dioxide and water. This is called photosynthesis. Animals cannot make their own food so they have to eat to get their energy. Some animals eat plants; these are known as **herbivores**. Some animals eat other animals and these are called **carnivores**. If an animal eats both plants and animals it is an **omnivore**.

A Food Chain

A plant (the wheat) captures the energy of the Sun by photosynthesis. This energy is stored in the wheat grains. When a herbivore (the mouse) eats the plant, the stored food energy can now be used by the herbivore. When a carnivore (the owl) eats the herbivore, the food energy is passed on again. Work out some food chains that you are part of. You should find that everything you eat depends at some point on the energy from the Sun.

A Food Chain Mobile

Copy the shapes of an owl, a mouse and a piece of grain onto cardboard, and then cut around the black lines. You should then have five separate pieces: a hollow owl, a hollow mouse, a piece of wheat and two eyes. To build the mobile, thread the pieces using a needle and thread as follows. Thread the wheat at W and hang it from the mouse at A. Thread the mouse at X and hang it from the owl at B. Thread the owl's eyes at Y (hang from C) and at Z (hang from D). Finally thread the owl at V so it can be hung up. Color the mobile before hanging it up.

Equipment: cardboard, scissors, thread, needle, paint or crayons.

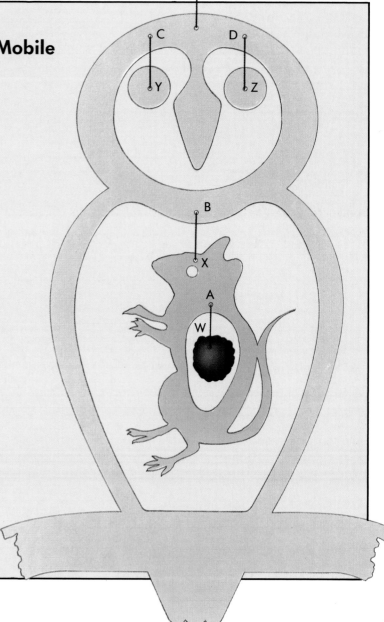

A Food Web

An owl does not only eat mice. It might also eat worms or small birds. A mouse might eat fruit as well as wheat. Small birds might eat worms, or fruit, or caterpillars. Draw and cut out pictures of various plants and animals. Try to link them into food chains. You will soon find that the foods are joined in a complicated web like the one below. Play this food web game. Make 20 yellow counters out of cardboard. Place these on the sun to represent the energy that comes from the sun.

Play the Game

On your own, or taking turns with someone else, move one counter at a time to one of the plants. You can now move any counter at any time — from sun to plant, from plant to animal, or from animal to animal. Counters can only be moved away from the sun, to show the movement of energy as food is eaten. If two or more counters reach one space, pile them up and then move them together. Keep moving counters until you have no more arrows to follow.

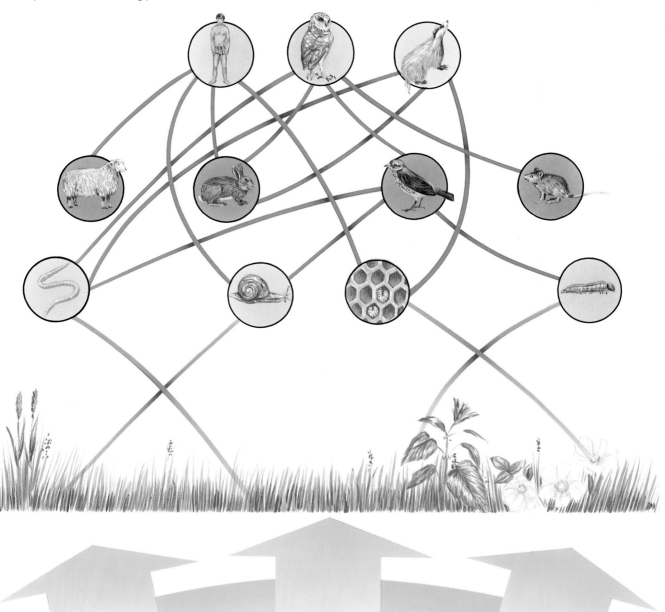

Survival

All living things need water. Green plants need sunlight to make food, while animals eat to get their energy. Some animals eat decaying matter, and are called **scavengers**. Vultures are scavengers. Sometimes food and light are hard to come by, so some plants and animals need to change their lifestyles in order to survive.

Surviving Drought

The driest places in the world are the deserts, for example the great Sahara. Very icy places are deserts too: there is plenty of water, but it is all locked up as ice. To survive drought, plants and animals need to be able to use quickly any rain that does fall. The spadefoot toad can exist without water in its burrow for months, but will emerge quickly if rain falls. A cactus in the desert will wait years for a rainshower, then suddenly it will flower.

Spadefoot toad

Bactrian camel

Cactus

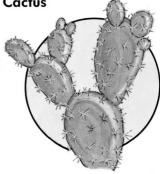

Eating to the Limit

Shrews have a constantly high demand for energy. Each day a shrew must eat its own weight in food — up to half an ounce. Imagine what this means. Weigh yourself, and then weigh out a 2 pounds of potatoes. Now calculate how many potatoes you would need to eat if you had to eat your own weight in food. The task is most difficult for shrews in the winter because there is a shortage of food and many die.

Bag of potatoes

Keeping Warm

Equipment: four identical jars with lids, hot water, themometer.

The experiment must be done on a cold day. Pour an equal amount of hot water from a pitcher into each of the four jars. Use the thermometer to check that the water is the same temperature in each jar. Now look around outside for good places to put one pot where it will hold its warmth. Put one of the pots out in the open and wrap another in

Both dormice (*above*) and bats (*below*) hibernate in the winter. Their body temperature can fall as low as 32°F.

The jar in the open will lose heat very quickly, like our unprotected skin would in cold places.

The jar with leaves around it will keep quite warm, though they do not insulate all that well.

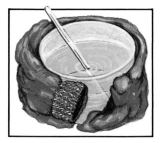

This jar will stay the warmest. The dry cloth provides good insulation much like an animal's coat.

A wet cloth will cool the water quickly. The evaporating water in the cloth draws heat from the water in the jar.

leaves. Put a wet cloth around one, and a dry one around another. After ten minutes, use the thermometer (or your little finger) to see which jars have kept their heat and which have gone cold. Keep checking the water at intervals to see which one stays hot the longest. Do you think you would have survived the winter?

How to Survive the Cold

The only way a shrew can survive cold winters is to keep eating to provide energy. Mammals and birds differ from other animals because much of their energy is used to keep themselves warm. One way some mammals save energy in the winter is to let their body become much cooler. This is rather like keeping the temperature in your house at 50°F instead of 70°F in the winter. A lot less fuel would be needed.

Outwitting the Winter

This game is best played with two or more people. One person becomes a swallow with a thin pointed beak (the paper clip). The other is a sparrow with a thicker beak (the clothespin). The foods on offer are seeds (the nuts) and soft creatures (the raisins). Use your "beak" to start "feeding," and store the food in front of you. In the summer both birds find insects best to eat. In the fall these run out, so the swallow **migrates**.

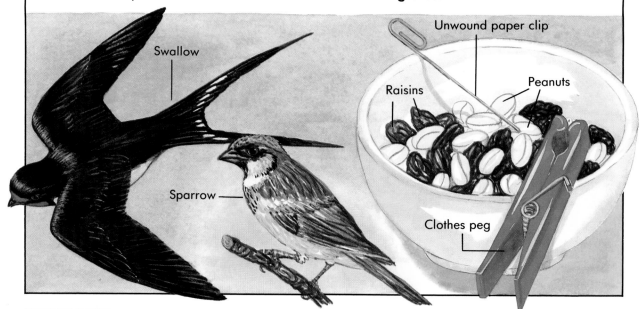

Swallow

Sparrow

Unwound paper clip

Raisins

Peanuts

Clothes peg

Sun Seekers

The body temperature of many creatures changes to match the temperature of the surroundings. Snakes and lizards sun themselves to increase their body temperature. Try this experiment in the summer to see if this is true for other creatures. Mark out 10 yards along a flower border. Walk slowly along this trail on a sunny day, noting how many insects there are. Do the same on a cool, cloudy day. Which creatures come out on the shady day?

Help a Bat

Equipment: You will need an adult to help with this. A plank of untreated wood 3 feet long, 8 inches wide, an inch thick, saw, nails, hammer.

The wood must never have been treated because the chemicals used might poison the bats. If it isn't rough, make grooves in it with the saw. Mark the plank as shown, and cut out the pieces. Nail the back through to the side pieces. Nail the top to the sides. Nail the front to the sides, beveling the top edge if possible to make a good fit. Nail in the bottom piece, leaving the gap against the back: this is where the bats will get in and out. Tack on some old rubber to seal between the back and lid. It is best to make three boxes and then space them around a tree trunk about 10 or 12 feet off the ground. The boxes can be nailed on but be careful as this can damage the tree.

You should not try to look in the box. Bats are very easily scared, and in some countries it is illegal to disturb them. Watch the box at dusk to see if any emerge, and look for tiny black droppings under the box. You may even be able to hear the high pitched squeak that the bats make as part of their echo location.

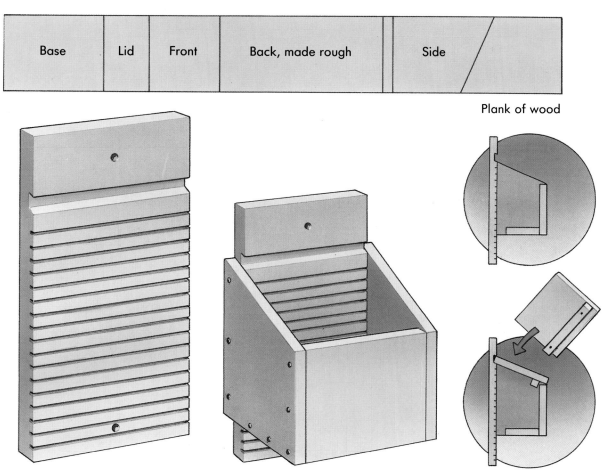

The grooves in the back of the box are for the bats to hang on to. When they rest bats hang upside down and need footholds, like those they would use in the wild.

Using nails to support the box can damage small trees. Another way of doing it is to use a length of old tire inner tube stretched through the box and around the tree.

Be very careful of disturbing the bats if they nest in your box. In many countries they are protected by law and disturbing nesting bats can be an offence.

Humans Helping Out

For some animals, staying alive, especially during the winter, can be a great problem. It is quite normal for many animals to die at this time of year. Many animals face extra problems because of the way humans behave. Here are some ways you can help animals to survive.

Make a Bird Table

Use a piece of outdoor plywood, about 20 × 12 inches and ¼ inch thick. Screw on thin wood strips from underneath to stop the seed blowing off, but leave gaps in the corners for drainage and cleaning. Attach the table to a post dug into the ground. Add some nails or hooks for hanging out nuts and bones. Paint with a non-toxic preservative and let it dry completely.

Clean it often with a stiff brush. If bird droppings build up around the base move the table occasionally.

Making Bird Pudding

This recipe for bird pudding is a good way of using up many kitchen scraps. Ask for a bowl of hot but not boiling water. Put a smaller bowl into the water and add the suet. Let it melt then stir in the scraps. Before the mixture hardens pour it into a yogurt cup or half a coconut shell. This should have had a hole made in the bottom and string threaded through. It can be hung up to attract the acrobatic birds, but for other birds you should put some of the mixture on a bird table.

Equipment: hot water in a bowl, equal amounts of suet and food or food scraps. The following may be used: bread, seeds, dried fruit, apples, bacon, oats. Do not use desiccated coconut or very salty foods.

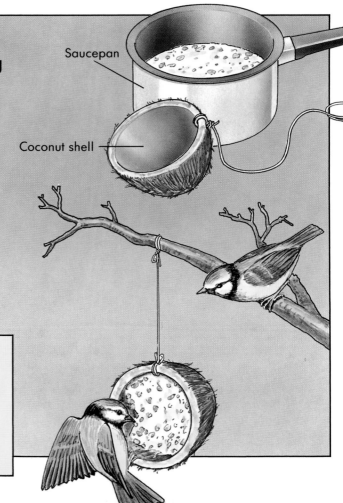

Saucepan

Coconut shell

Make a Nut Holder

Equipment: plastic bottle, string, scissors, peanuts.

Ask an adult to make two holes in the bottom of the bottle, on opposite sides. Thread string through these so the bottle can be hung upside down. Draw a line around the bottle about half way up. Ask for about ten holes to be made along this. Use these to cut slits down the bottle. Funnel the peanuts in through the top and replace the lid. Hang the bottle up. If the birds can't get a grip, push a stick right through two opposite slits.

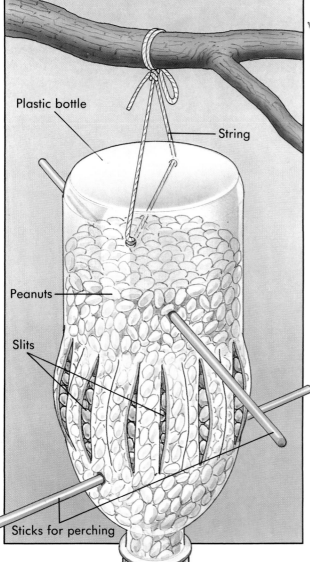

Plastic bottle

String

Peanuts

Slits

Sticks for perching

Helping With Housing

Often gardens and parks are too tidy for insects to find food and make a home. You can help by asking to have a small wild corner by a fence or hedge. Put down logs and flat stones. Let the grass grow up, and make sure the area isn't sprayed. The minibeasts that make a home here will in turn provide food for larger animals.

Bathtime

Bird baths are useful all through the year. An old lid is fine, or a tray, but the inside must be rough and not slippery. Put a few stones in and make sure to change the water daily. If it freezes, melt it with warm water. Birds will drink in it, and also bathe to keep their feathers in good shape.

Index

Editors: Thomas Keegan and
Annabel Warburg
Designer: Ben White
Illustrators: Kuo Kang Chen ●
Cecilia Fitzsimmons

Additional Illustrations: *Oxford Illustrators
pages 28–29, 32–33*
Cover Design: *Terry Woodley*
Picture Research: *Elaine Willis*

*The publishers wish to thank the following for
supplying photographs for this book:*

*Page 4 Rosie Harlow; 13 ZEFA; 15 Rosie Harlow; 20
ZEFA; 25 Nature Photographers; 27 Rosie Harlow; 31
NHPA/R.Tidman (top), ZEFA (bottom); 35 Dr. Robert
Stebbings.*

Published in 1991 by Warwick Press,
387 Park Avenue South, New York, New York, 10016.
First published in 1991 by Kingfisher Books.
Copyright © Grisewood & Dempsey Ltd. 1991.

6 5 4 3 2 1
All rights reserved
Printed in Hong Kong

Library of Congress Cataloging-in-Publication Data
Harlow, Rosie
   Energy and growth / Rosie Harlow and Gareth
   Morgan
      p.   cm. — (Fun with science)
   Includes index.
   Summary: Suggests with which to investigate such
aspects of life as food chains, hibernation, life cycles,
and specialized food and habitats.
   ISBN 0–531–19124–9
   1. Biology—Experiments—Juvenile literature.
   2. Ecology— Experiments—Juvenile literature.
   (1. Biology—Experiments. 2. Ecology—Experiments.
   3. Experiments.)
   I. Morgan, Gareth   II. Title.   III. Series.
   QH316.5.M67   1991   91–9570
   574.5′078—dc20   CIP
                                             AC

93-929